SNAKES ON A PLANE

SNAKES ON A PLANE

The Complete Quote Book

Screenplay by John Heffernan and Sebastian Gutierrez
Story by David Dalessandro and John Heffernan
Snake Bites by David Jacobs

HARPER

NEW YORK • LONDON • TORONTO • SYDNEY

HarperCollins books may be purchased for educational, business, or sales promotional use. For information please write: Special Markets Department, HarperCollins Publishers Inc., 10 East 53rd Street, New York, NY 10022.

FIRST EDITION

Designed by Joel Avirom, Jason Snyder, and Meghan Day Healey

Library of Congress Cataloging-in-Publication Data has been applied for.

ISBN-10: 0-06-123886-4
ISBN-13: 978-0-06-123886-4

06 07 08 09 10 ❖/RRD 10 9 8 7 6 5 4 3 2 1

"HOW DID YOU IMBECILES LET SOMEBODY TRANSPORT SNAKES ON A PASSENGER FLIGHT?!?"

CONTENTS

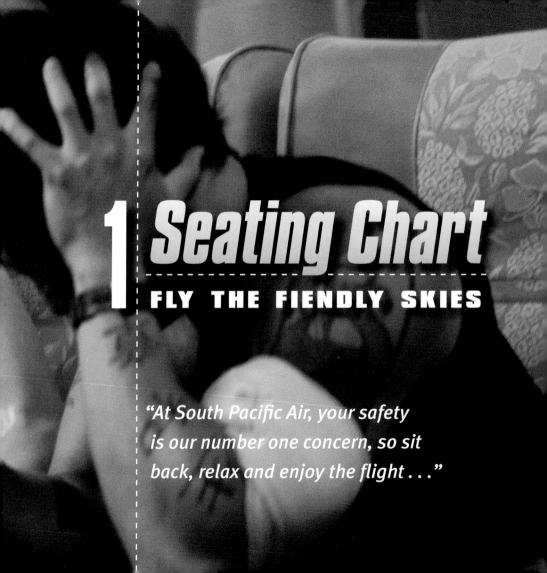

1 *Seating Chart*

FLY THE FIENDLY SKIES

"At South Pacific Air, your safety is our number one concern, so sit back, relax and enjoy the flight . . ."

PACIFIC AIR FLIGHT 121

Crew

- - - - - - - - - - - - - - - - - - - -

CAPTAIN SAM McKEON: Your pilot on a flight into nightmare

CO-PILOT RICK: He chose the wrong day to wear his snakeskin boots

CLAIRE MILLER, FLIGHT ATTENDANT: Coffee, Tea or Anti-venom?

TIFFANY, FLIGHT ATTENDANT: Comely sky candy—care to take a bite out of her?

KEN, FLIGHT ATTENDANT: Don't be fooled by that twinkle in his eye—several snakes did, to their everlasting regret.

GRACE, FLIGHT ATTENDANT: Maybe she should have taken that early retirement plan after all

Passengers (The Warm-blooded Variety)

SEAN JONES: Surfer dude who's really gonna take it to the extreme

NEVILLE FLYNN: FBI Special Agent and Public Enemy Number One in Snakeville

JOHN SANDERS: Flynn's partner, who suffers from a fear of snakes

THREE G's: This germ-phobic rap artist is the Howard Hughes of hip-hop

BIG LEROY: To Three G's, a bodyguard; to a snake, prime beef walking

TROY: Another bodyguard, whose 2,000 hours on a flight simulator video game just might pay off

MERCEDES: Airhead heiress who thinks getting bumped from First Class to Coach is the worst thing that's going to happen on Flight 121

MARY-KATE: Mercedes' toy dog and a toothsome morsel for some lucky snake

TYLER and ASHLEY: Newlyweds who should've honeymooned on the mainland

MARIA: Single mother with child—Caution! Baby on board!

PAUL: Uptight asshole executive slated for a whole lot of Maalox moments

KYLE and KELLY: Overheated young lovers who go from the Mile High Club to the Mile Die Club

CHEN LEONG: Martial artist whose Snake Fist fighting technique is gonna come in handy this trip

MRS. BOVA: A whole lotta woman with a hot date with a whole lotta snake

CURTIS and TOMMY: Youngsters taking their first flight without parental supervision; what could go wrong?

Passengers (The Cold-blooded Variety)

TAIPAN: Mean-tempered brute who draws first blood—and last?

PIT VIPER: His strategy was simple—if the pilot is bitten, he can't fly the plane.

MULGA: Tree-climbing snake who likes to climb more than just trees

EYELASH VIPER: Neat, petite, and nastily venomous

COPPERHEAD: She strikes straight at the "seat" of the problem

MONOCLED COBRA: So classy, he only bites passengers flying in First Class

BURMESE PYTHON: He's huge, with an appetite to match

BLACK MAMBA: So ill-tempered, she'd bite herself if she could

GREEN MAMBA: The original snake in the grass; he's pretty good in a cockpit, too

NORTH AMERICAN RATTLESNAKE: Homegrown hero; that is, if you happen to be a serpent

Earthbound

EDDIE KIM: Vicious crime lord who says "Murder" with a mess of snakes

HANK HARRIS: The FBI's man in charge on the ground in Los Angeles

EMMETT BRADLEY: Supervisor on duty at LAX Air Control Tower

DR. STEVEN PRICE: This renowned snake expert's due for a busy night

KRAITLER: Smuggler of exotic animals who booked a big bunch of killer snakes on Pacific Air 121

VENEZUELAN RATTLESNAKE: He missed the plane but got in on some of the action

2 Pre-Flight

Brutal Murder!

HAWAIIAN NEWS ANCHOR: This is Mi Jung Lee reporting live from the Kaena Point area. Details remain sketchy regarding the brutal slaying yesterday of Los Angeles Prosecutor Daniel Hayes who was vacationing in Hawaii. Hayes has been in the news for his high profile pursuit of reputed mobster Edward Kim.... The ongoing saga in the criminal investigation of Mr. Kim has involved charges of murder and racketeering, as well as police corruption at the highest levels both here in Hawaii and on the Mainland . . .

Snake Bite There are close to three thousand different species of snakes in the world, and all of them are carnivorous. All snakes are predators, their prey ranging in size from insects up to small four-legged mammals and beyond, rarely—but sometimes—also including humans. There's no such thing as a vegetarian snake.

Guardian Angel

Sean Jones witnessed Eddie Kim's murder of Prosecutor Hayes. Now, Kim's thugs are closing in on Sean, when FBI Agent Neville Flynn comes to the rescue.

FLYNN (to Sean): Do as I say, you live.

Snake Bite Experts say that the best way to avoid getting bitten when walking through snake country is to wear hiking boots and shun sandals and bare feet. Or you could just stay the hell away from there in the first place.

Reluctant Witness

FLYNN: He knows you saw him. That's why his thugs were at your apartment. Make no mistake, Eddie Kim will kill you—if you let him.

SEAN: You make it sound like I have no choice. Last week I'm planning a surfing trip to Bali and now . . .

FLYNN: Oh, you have choices. That's just it. But only one choice is the right one. Come to L.A. with me, testify and put this bastard away for life. . . . Think it through, I'll be outside.

Snake Bite

In the game of craps, when a pair of dice come up with one dot showing on each face, the combination is called "snake eyes." The shooter loses the throw and the bet and is said to have "crapped out."

3 Boarding

You Can't Always Get What You Want

Flight Attendants Claire, Tiffany, and Grace head for the Flight 121 departure gate. Claire will be leaving her job to become a lawyer.

TIFFANY: So, any requests for your final flight?

CLAIRE: Only what any Flight Attendant wants.

CLAIRE and TIFFANY (in unison): Low-maintenance passengers.

CLAIRE: . . . I'm going to miss night flights.

GRACE: Yeah. I enjoy passengers so much more when they're unconscious.

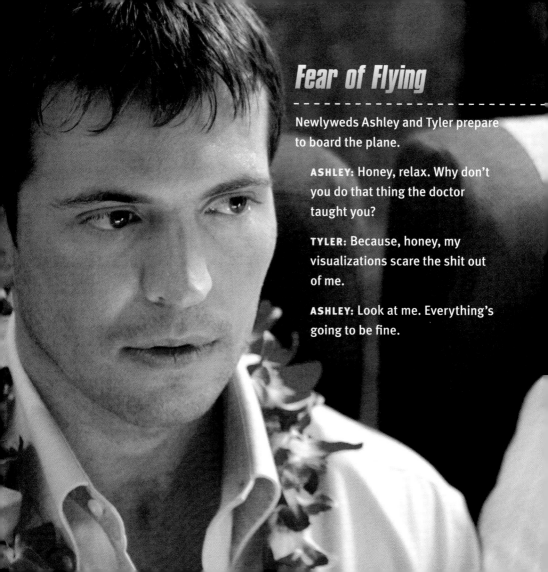

Fear of Flying

Newlyweds Ashley and Tyler prepare to board the plane.

ASHLEY: Honey, relax. Why don't you do that thing the doctor taught you?

TYLER: Because, honey, my visualizations scare the shit out of me.

ASHLEY: Look at me. Everything's going to be fine.

Snake Bite In 2006, in the Florida Everglades, a python was found dead with a dead alligator inside it. The python had swallowed the 'gator whole, causing its belly to explode. Did somebody say something about "biting off more than it can chew"?

Alligators are native to the region but not pythons. The snake is believed to have been imported, most likely illegally— a "pet" whose owner might have turned it loose in the swamp when it got too big to keep around the house.

Snake Bite One of the leading causes of death in India is snakebite. In Bombay alone, a thousand people a year die from it. So, whoever those folks are, they should leave town.

23

Top Priority

CAPTAIN McKEON: FBI's escorting some guy to L.A. They just took over all of First Class.

CLAIRE: Are they allowed to do that?

CAPT. McKEON: Well, apparently FAA section 108 states that if deemed necessary, they can do whatever they want.

CLAIRE: So who gets to tell all the paying First Class passengers they'll be flying Coach?

CAPT. McKEON: That'd be you, kid.

Snake Bite A popular war flag of the American Revolution depicted a snake made up of thirteen segments, representing the original thirteen colonies. The flag bore the motto, "Don't tread on me."

Smooth Talk

Co-pilot Rick joins Claire, Grace and Tiffany in the galley. He's wearing gaudy snakeskin boots.

RICK (to Claire): I was hoping you'd be the sky candy on this flight. You're looking especially delicious today.

CLAIRE: I love it when you demean me, Rick.

RICK: My pleasure.

Snake Bite

Snakes are lizards without limbs, though in some cases, tiny vestigial spurs still remain. Sometimes these spurs are used during mating, when they are inserted into the female's orifice to heighten the intensity of the love-play.

4 Getting Acquainted

Snake Bite All snakes are deaf. Having no ears, they hear no sounds. They are extraordinarily sensitive to vibrations and olfactory stimuli. Some are equipped with infrared-sensitive pits, which can "see" heat. This makes them fully functional hunter-killers even in the dark—a useful talent when the lights go out. Especially on an airplane.

Uptight Bizman Part 1

CLAIRE: Unfortunately First Class has been overbooked, but there's plenty of room to stretch out in Coach, which is less than half full. For the inconvenience, we're giving you a Free Travel Coupon good on any South Pacific Air flight.

PAUL: A Free Travel Coupon doesn't help me get to my meeting on time, now does it?

CLAIRE: Sir, I'm pretty sure Coach will get to Los Angeles about the same time as First.

PAUL: Funny. Does my Platinum Awards Membership include free sarcasm or should I take that up with your supervisor?

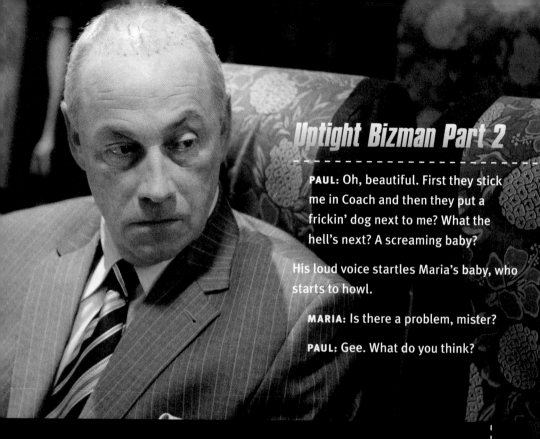

Uptight Bizman Part 2

PAUL: Oh, beautiful. First they stick me in Coach and then they put a frickin' dog next to me? What the hell's next? A screaming baby?

His loud voice startles Maria's baby, who starts to howl.

MARIA: Is there a problem, mister?

PAUL: Gee. What do you think?

Snake Bite We all have a snake brain inside us. Called the limbic region, and located in the mid-brain, it's one of the most ancient and primitive cerebral structures, an evolutionary heritage from our reptilian forebears. It's the part of the brain most involved with the basic drives of life: fight or flight, aggression, fear, food and mating.

That's Hot

TIFFANY: Mind if I ask what you did?

SEAN: Me? Nothing. It's what I'm supposed to do. Ever hear of Eddie Kim?

TIFFANY: Who hasn't? I saw one of those crime shows once with the hokey reenactments where he tortured this guy who was a witness against him by gouging out his eyes and then feeding him to some pigs. Gruesome stuff.

SEAN: Yeah. He doesn't mess around, that guy.

Snake Bite

Snakes have no eyelids. Their eyes are protected by transparent scales, which cover them like goggles. They do not blink, which helps intensify the celebrated illusion of their "hypnotic" stare, which is said to paralyze its victim. In reality, what really freezes the prey is its stark terror at the presence of the snake.

Keep Your Sexy Right

THREE G's (to Mercedes): So I have to pay attention to everything from finding the right accountant to making sure I look fit and fine, because keeping my sexy right is part of the business, too. And if you don't mind me saying, it looks like you keep your sexy very, very right. . . . Have you ever acted? Because you'd be great in one of my pool-party videos.

Snake Bite It's not the music of the snake charmer's flute that keeps the snake from biting him. Having no ears, snakes hear no music, no sounds. It's been suggested that the charmer's hand movements and rhythmic swayings entrance the snake. Is the snake fascinated or simply playing along, biding his time and waiting for the right opportunity to sink his fangs into the charmer? Talk about playing to a tough audience!

5 *First Contact*

Trojan Horse

- -

Flynn explores the plane's cargo hold. Luggage is strewn about along with boxes of leis and flowers scattered everywhere. He communicates with Claire in First Class via a two-way radio handset.

FLYNN: Flowers. Boxes of them. Scattered all over the place.

He picks one up. "Aloha Kingdom Flowers and Gifts" is stenciled on its side.

CLAIRE: What do you mean?

FLYNN: Nice touch. That's how they got the snakes aboard. . . . Then they jammed open an access door to make sure the snakes would make it out of the cargo bay.

Scent of Murder

Snake expert Dr. Price interrogates Kraitler, the smuggler and mass murderer who packed the cargo of deadly serpents on Flight 121.

DR. PRICE: How did you get the snakes to be so aggressive?

KRAITLER: Pheromone . . . we sprayed the leis with it so that the plane's air system would circulate it throughout. I swear to God. That's it!

Personality Profile
TAIPAN

Taipan is a *badass*.

Nine feet long with wicked yellow eyes, he lives up to the species' reputation as one of the world's deadliest snakes, and revels in it! In the anti-human onslaught aboard Flight 121, he draws first blood and keeps right in there pitching until the finish, craving the honor of the final kill.

If Taipan could speak, he might say something like this:

"I am feared and respected in my native land. My venom is so potent it could drop a water buffalo dead in its tracks. If you want to live, give me a wide berth, because I'll go out of my way to sink my fangs in somebody, anybody, just for the hell of it. That's the kind of snake that I am."

Snake Bite Found mostly in Australia and the island of New Guinea, the taipan is a member of the elapid family, which also contains the cobra and the mamba. Snakes have fangs either in the front or the back of the mouth; elapids have them in the front. The taipan is rated as one of the world's most dangerous venomous snakes. Luckily for the race of men, the taipan is relatively rare and secretive.

Snake Bite Snakes have a highly developed sense of smell. In addition to its nostrils, the snake's forked, flickering tongue collects scent molecules, which are then perceived by olfactory chambers inside its mouth called Jacobson's organ. During the mating season, female snakes emit powerful sex pheromones, scents which attract the males and enhance the urge to merge.

Hello, Young Lovers— and Goodbye

Kelly and Kyle are getting it on in the lavatory when Taipan strikes. Ken and Grace hear screaming from within the bathroom.

KEN: Mile High Club.

GRACE: Ah, those were the days. . . . This guy's really good.

In an instant, the screaming and commotion stop.

GRACE: Well, maybe not that good.

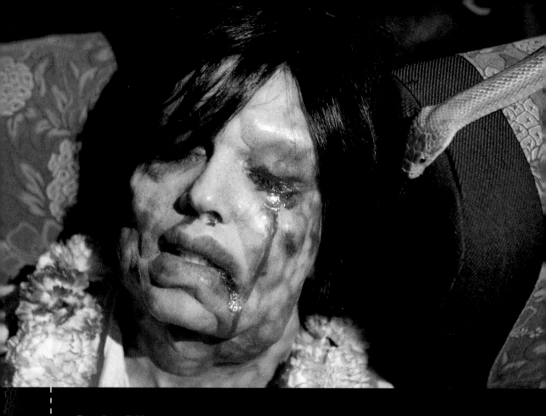

Snake Bite The fang of a venomous snake is like a hypodermic needle. It's hollow and terminates in a point as sharp as a pin. Venom is pumped from the sacks through a tiny hole in the tooth and injected into the flesh of the prey, inducing shock, paralysis and sometimes death.

Snake Bite

Snakes are generally immune to other snakes' venom. Call it "professional courtesy."

Only a small proportion of all snakes are dangerous to humans. Of course, those are the species that are on the plane.

Flying Blind

Pit Viper tangles with a live wire inside the instrument panel, shorting it out and crashing the entire computerized display. Every digital instrument necessary to fly the plane turns pitch black.

RICK (into radio): LAX, Hula one-two-one. May Day. We are fifteen hundred nautical miles southwest of LAX. Repeat, May Day. We are in distress.

6 Turbulence

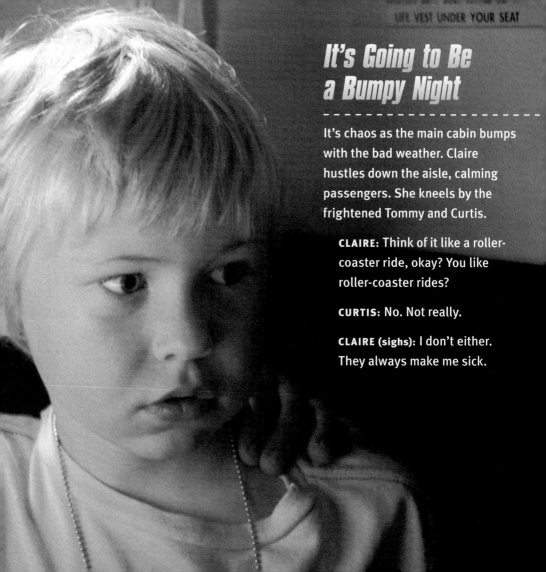

LIFE VEST UNDER YOUR SEAT

It's Going to Be a Bumpy Night

It's chaos as the main cabin bumps with the bad weather. Claire hustles down the aisle, calming passengers. She kneels by the frightened Tommy and Curtis.

CLAIRE: Think of it like a roller-coaster ride, okay? You like roller-coaster rides?

CURTIS: No. Not really.

CLAIRE (sighs): I don't either. They always make me sick.

Uh-oh

Pit Viper fangs Captain McKeon and slithers away. Claire looks down the hatchway to see McKeon collapse into a motionless clump.

CLAIRE: Captain?! Rick, the captain's not moving!

RICK: Christ, he must've had a heart attack. . . . Jesus, I flew with him for ten years.

Snake Bite

Humans are born with two innate fears: fear of falling, and the fear of snakes. These fears are hard-wired into our brains, encoded into our DNA, an inheritance from the primitive tree-dwelling apes who were our distant ancestors. To them, a fall was disastrous if not fatal, while the predator most to be feared were massive, tree-climbing snakes of a type mercifully long-since extinct.

To be trapped on a plane high up in mid-air with a horde of snakes, therefore, taps into both of these primal fears. Next time, take the boat.

Personality Profile

PIT VIPER

Pit Viper is the super-trooper of the snake brigade. He hits the human enemy right where it hurts, at the top of the chain of command.

Pit Viper is on a recon mission inside the cockpit instrument panel when he bumps his head against a hot electronics board, crashing a whole lot of fancy avionics equipment. Sustaining painful and disfiguring facial burns that would have stopped a less determined snake, Pit Viper continues on his mission of vengeance.

Aiming straight for the top, he targets the humans' Most Valuable Player, airplane pilot Captain Sam McKeon, zeroing in on him like a heat-seeking missile with a lethal payload of toxic venom.

Not content to rest on his laurels, Pit Viper then sets his fangs for co-pilot Rick.

Trying for a trifecta, he attacks Flight Attendant Claire Miller.

Trouble is, Claire's on a mission, too—and she's armed with an ax.

Snake Bite When one says of a viper, "It's the pits," it's not a put-down but a compliment. Scientists tell us that the pit viper is the most highly evolved of snakes—"highly evolved" being defined here as a more efficient killing machine. Pits are sensory organs that detect heat; organic thermal imaging units. Located in the snake's head, they enable the pit viper to "see" its prey by the infrared body heat it emits. A live human's body temperature of 98.6 degrees must register like a bonfire on a viper's pits. Apart from vipers, boas and pythons also possess pits.

Deadlier Than the Male

FLYNN: Hey, law school doesn't work out, you're pretty good with that ax.

CLAIRE: Yeah, you think you've forgotten how to fight giant snakes but then it all comes back to you.

Personality Profile
MULGA

Mulga? He could have just as easily been named "Cuddles." He only wants to make nice. Snakes love warm, enclosed spaces, so when Mulga happens upon the sleeping Mrs. Bova, he just has to react.

Also known as the King Brown Snake, the Mulga is an elapid, a member of the same family as the cobra, mamba and krait. It's found throughout Australia, thriving in habitats as diverse as rain forests or deserts. It's a tree-climbing snake—a hell of a note for unsuspecting monkeys and nesting birds.

Now, a human limb is no more difficult to climb than a tree limb, especially when the human in question is fast asleep, as is Mrs. Bova. Doing what comes naturally, Mulga entwines himself around one of her legs and slithers up to the top of it and under her dress. And then—wouldn't you know it?—she wakes up and sees his head sticking up from her bosom, playing peek-a-boo.

The Greeks Had a Word for It

Flynn hauls a stricken Sanders out of a mess of snakes.
Sanders clings to Flynn, barely breathing.

SANDERS: Since I was a kid . . . Ophidi—Ophidi—
Ophidiaphobia—

FLYNN: John, I don't know what that is.

SANDERS: Fear. Of. Snakes.

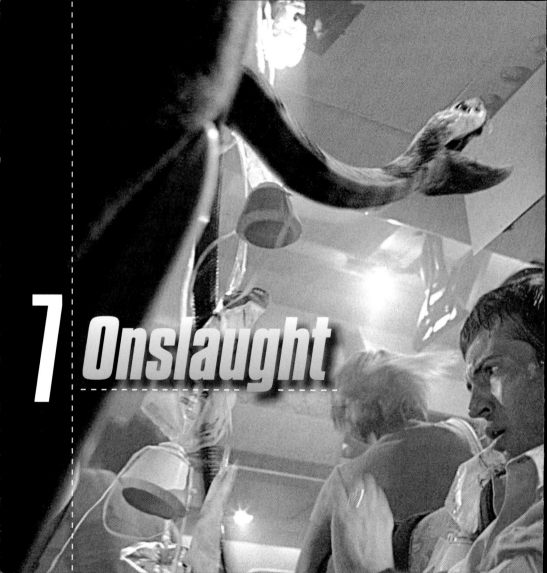

7 Onslaught

SSSSSSSSaboteurs!

RICK: Sorry about the bumpy ride, doll, but you are not going to believe what came out of the goddamn instrument panel.

He holds up a deceased Eyelash Viper, smashed flat as a fried egg.

RICK: Have you ever seen anything like this in your life?

Counterattack

Ken splashes hot pots of coffee on the heads of attacking snakes.

KEN: TASTE THIS, YOU BITCHES!

FLYNN: We need weapons. Where is the silverware?

CLAIRE: There isn't any. All we have are these.

She holds up the dull-edged utensils known as—

FLYNN: Sporks?

Personality Profile
EYELASH VIPER

Jeepers, creepers, where'd you get those peepers?!

Eyelash Viper gets that a lot because he's a proud member of a unique species with a distinctive signature look. He, like all his kind, sports what looks like thick, curling eyelashes rimming the tops of his beady eyes. Actually, they're not lashes at all, but scaly, fringelike protuberances.

Eyelash Vipers are tree-dwelling snakes found in Central and South American jungles and rain forests. Their coloring ranges from solid yellow to more subdued greens and browns. Modest-sized, they generally grow no larger than two feet long.

They're petite, pencil-thin and pert, but don't let those dandified looks fool you. When push comes to shove, they're still vipers and their venom packs a wallop equivalent to getting hit on the head with a concrete block.

Eyelash Viper and his associates serve the cause by acting as what could be called "advance men," or rather, "advance snakes." They steal into the cockpit, triggering an electrical short that deploys the emergency oxygen masks in the main cabin, opening the way for a mass snake assault on the passengers.

Proving again that it's not the size of the fighter, but the size of the fight that's in him that counts.

This Sucks

Big Leroy's been bitten in the behind by Penny the Copperhead. Ken looks to Troy from where he's cutting open the back of Leroy's pants to expose the wound.

KEN: We have to suck out the poison.

TROY: I ain't suckin' nothing.

KEN: OK, I'll do it.

BIG LEROY: WHOA! There'll be no sucking! Get this man away from my ass!

Hurting

Big Leroy coughs in pain.

TROY (to Claire): You've got to give my boy something for the pain.

CLAIRE: We're doing everything we can, sir.

GRACE: The passengers are right. These seats are really uncomfortable.

Personality Profile
COPPERHEAD

Copperhead proves that you don't have to go abroad to exotic, distant climes to be menaced by killer snakes; you can experience the same blood-runs-cold sense of naked fear right in your own backyard.

You can, that is, if you live in the eastern part of the United States or in New Mexico.

Copperheads are irritable by nature, and the buffeting and chaos they've experienced in midair on Flight 121 is not of the kind to lull them into a sense of genial good nature.

For Copperhead, the sight of Big Leroy's fat ass wriggling around in front of her face is like waving a red flag at a bull. She just has to have a piece of that, so she does what any self-respecting copperhead would do—she strikes!

- -

Snake Bite
The copperhead is a stout, burly pit viper with a wedge-shaped head. It bears markings of bands of lighter tans and pinks alternating with darker bands of red and brown.

One of its preferred habitats is among piles of rocks, as hikers who cross stone fences and walls occasionally discover to their dismay. The copperhead is found largely on the eastern seaboard of the United States, though not in Florida (perhaps it wished to avoid the boredom of an early retirement).

8 Sky Siege

Personality Profile
MONOCLE COBRA

Monocle Cobra brings something to the party that money can't buy: *class*.

After all, who wears a monocle nowadays? The whole species of Thai Monoculate Cobras, that's who.

This dangerous, highly venomous snake is found in Thailand and Vietnam. Monocle Cobras are distinguished by a single black marking on the back of the hood. They're not to be confused with their cousins, the Indian Spectacled Cobra, who have a spectacle-shaped pair of black markings on the backs of their hoods.

(The cobra's hood is a kind of defense mechanism. When threatened, the ribbed hood expands, increasing the snake's size and serving as a warning to deter potential foes.)

Monocle Cobras sure aren't picky eaters. They're cannibalistic and will eat smaller members of their own species.

Snake Bite The spitting cobra was long thought to be a myth, a creature out of folklore—a belief generally held by those who made their homes a long distance from Malaysia, Indonesia, and parts of East and South Africa, where varieties of the breed are found. African spitters include the East African Rinkhal and the Mozambique Spitting Cobra.

The snake spits—with deadly accuracy—a stream of venom through holes in its fangs, a spray with a reach of from six to eight feet. It aims for the face of its target, and the spray can cause blindness.

First Aid: The Basics

Tommy and Curtis are huddled together in the forward galley. Tommy is barely conscious, his arm is horribly swollen.

CURTIS: Mister? My brother, he got bit. . . . I was supposed to take care of him.

FLYNN: I know the basics. Drain the venom, clean the wounds, wrap tourniquets between the wound and the heart, and stay calm.

Worth a Thousand Words

Dr. Price checks Tommy's wound, unsure of what anti-venom to use.

> **DR. PRICE:** Anyone see the snake that bit him?

> **CURTIS:** We couldn't find the snake that bit him so I drew a picture.

Curtis hands Price the picture he drew of the snake.

> **DR. PRICE:** A Cobra?

Snake Bite The slim, deadly King Cobra has been known to reach a length of fifteen to eighteen feet, making it the world's longest venomous snake. It's found in India, Southeast Asia and the Phillipines.

Shunning human habitations, the King prefers to live in remote forests and other isolated locales. It lives on a diet of other snakes. Apparently, among cobras as in humans, that's how you get to be the king—by eating the competition.

Personality Profile
BLACK MAMBA

It's hard to be Number One, but the black mamba has risen to the challenge of being the most venomous snake in all of Africa. No mean feat, considering the competition: the Nile cobra, the West African bush viper, the Rinkhal spitting cobra, and many others.

The black mamba's habitat includes grasslands and forests; it's equally at home on the ground or in the trees. Oddly, the black mamba is generally dark gray or lead-colored; the inside of its mouth is black.

Be very clear: The mambo is a Latin dance step. The mamba is a venomous, bad-tempered snake, and Black Mamba is a mamba's mamba. Her venom is an incredibly potent toxin. When she puts the bite on a man, swiftly and inevitably he finds himself in a dance of death.

Illustrating the maxim that power corrupts, Mamba is also incredibly belligerent, ready to take on all comers as she slithers through the jungle with a chip on her shoulder.

She's spoiling for a fight, and she's going to get one. Tonight, on Pacific Air Flight 121, she will contend with martial artist Chen Leong!

The prize: the life of the lovely Mercedes.

Snake Bite Many Kung Fu techniques were developed centuries ago in China by careful observation of different animal fighting styles. The Snake Fist fighting style was inspired by the quick and deadly accurate lunges of a snake striking at its prey.

The Lowdown

Flynn speaks to Agent Harris in L.A.

FLYNN: Kim somehow loaded the plane with deadly snakes.

HARRIS: What kind of insane plan is that? He can't possibly guarantee a snake will get to Sean—

FLYNN: Doesn't have to guarantee it if he brings the whole plane down.

Snake Bite

Actually, snakes are not slimy. They are dry to the touch.

Game Plan?

FLYNN: Alright. Let's figure out what to do.

RICK: I know what I have to do. We're in a two hundred foot aluminum tube at thirty thousand feet and any one of those little slimy pieces of shit can trip a circuit, a relay system or a hydraulic and this bird goes down faster than a Thai hooker. So my job is to keep LAX up-to-date on how totally SCREWED we are, then find some way to keep this mother up in the sky another two hours.

He stabs a finger at Flynn.

RICK: Figure *that* out.

9 Second Wave

NORTH AMERICAN RATTLESNAKE

Let's hear it for the good old U.S.A., which produces not only the rugged, versatile copperhead but also the rattlesnake, a species which embodies the spirit of fair play and sportsmanship that made this country great.

And let's hear it for North American Rattlesnake, a fine, upstanding rattler and a credit to his breed.

Snake Bite The rattlesnake's rattle is a remnant of the skins it has shed. Each time it sheds, another ring is added to the rattle. A rattlesnake's age can be determined by the number of rings on its rattle, if the rattle is intact and has never been broken.

Domestic varieties of this successful and far-flung breed include the Timber Rattlesnake, the Eastern Diamondback, Western Diamondback, Western Rattlesnake, and the desert-dwelling Sidewinder.

North American Rattlesnake comes equipped with his own warning system. When he sounds his rattle, he's saying: *Beware! I'm trouble!*

That means you better back off—fast.

When he stops rattling, though, is when you've really got to worry, because that means that he's about to strike.

North American Rattlesnake brings a potent hellbrew of venom to the party. Rattlesnake venom contains a digestive agent which breaks down the tissues of its prey, wreaking great destruction. Sometimes the damage is so bad, there's nothing to be done but to amputate.

Personality Profile
NORTH AMERICAN RATTLESNAKE

Let's hear it for the good old U.S.A., which produces not only the rugged, versatile copperhead but also the rattlesnake, a species which embodies the spirit of fair play and sportsmanship that made this country great.

And let's hear it for North American Rattlesnake, a fine, upstanding rattler and a credit to his breed.

Snake Bite

The rattlesnake's rattle is a remnant of the skins it has shed. Each time it sheds, another ring is added to the rattle. A rattlesnake's age can be determined by the number of rings on its rattle, if the rattle is intact and has never been broken.

Domestic varieties of this successful and far-flung breed include the Timber Rattlesnake, the Eastern Diamondback, Western Diamondback, Western Rattlesnake, and the desert-dwelling Sidewinder.

North American Rattlesnake comes equipped with his own warning system. When he sounds his rattle, he's saying: *Beware! I'm trouble!*

That means you better back off—fast.

When he stops rattling, though, is when you've really got to worry, because that means that he's about to strike.

North American Rattlesnake brings a potent hellbrew of venom to the party. Rattlesnake venom contains a digestive agent which breaks down the tissues of its prey, wreaking great destruction. Sometimes the damage is so bad, there's nothing to be done but to amputate.

72

Snake Bite In the frontier days of the American West, unscrupulous vendors would "spike" their rotgut whiskey by dropping rattlesnake heads into each barrel. (In addition to steeping it with horse manure to color it.) The standard dosage was usually about six heads per barrel. The residual venom would give the raw whiskey a real kick. The practice was so common that the term "six-snake whiskey" came into popular use to describe any kind of bad or foul liquor.

Spit, Don't Swallow

Snake Bite

Experts tend to discourage the practice of amateurs in the field trying to give first aid to snake bite victims by sucking the poison from the wound. The danger is that the sucker will accidentally swallow some venom, resulting in two emergency cases instead of one.

They suggest using a tourniquet above the wounded area instead. Of course, that doesn't count for extreme emergencies, like snakes getting loose in an airplane in mid-flight. Up there, all bets are off. You take your chances and use what works. Try not to swallow!

The Expert

At the UCLA Zoology Building, Agent Harris
intercepts Dr. Price.

HARRIS: Dr. Price?

DR. PRICE: Yes?

HARRIS: I'm Agent Harris.

DR. PRICE: Sure hope this is important. I've
got baby Antiguan racer eggs in there ready
to hatch. It'll be the first time in captivity.
Very exciting.

HARRIS: Really? Well, I have another exciting
"first" I'd like to tell you about.

At Least It Wasn't Meth

Flynn and Dr. Price use a comm unit to dialogue.

DR. PRICE: Snakes don't attack unless they're threatened. Something's provoking them.

FLYNN: No shit . . . they're going after everybody. Even the goddamn leis . . . they wrap their crazy ass selves all over them.

DR. PRICE: The leis? Jesus . . . I don't know . . . It . . . it could possibly be a pheromone. That's what female animals release to trigger mating behavior. It can also provoke serious hyper-aggression . . . like some kind of drug.

FLYNN: Great. Snakes on crack.

Snake Bite Due to its practice of shedding its skin, the snake was thought to be immortal by many of the folk of antiquity. Snake cults center around the themes of rebirth and resurrection.

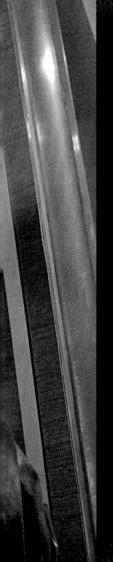

Picture This

Flynn radios Dr. Price to try to determine what kind of snake bit Big Leroy.

> **FLYNN:** Okay, we got one here that's black on top, green on bottom.

> **DR. PRICE:** Pure green? Or is there blue?

> **FLYNN (confused):** Mostly green, I guess—

> **KEN:** TEAL! It's a deep shade of teal.

Snake Bite
The anaconda flourishes in the Amazon jungle, where it can grow to a length of twenty feet or more.

Stories persist of anacondas deep in the interior that reach a length of forty feet or more, but no one has ever brought a specimen back to civilization. Perhaps the discoverers—if any—of the giant anaconda became the prey rather than the hunter, and were instead taken to the legendary creature's lair, carried within the belly of the beast.

10 Nightmare Vector

Doggie Treat

Burmese Python zeroes in on Paul. Paul grabs Mary-Kate and tosses her at the creature. The small dog disappears down Burmese Python's gullet, who then slithers behind some seats, disappearing from view.

MERCEDES: MARY-KATE!!!

MERCEDES (to Paul): You animal! How could you do that?

PAUL: Oh come on! You all would have done the exact same thing! It's a frickin' dog, people.

Personality Profile
BURMESE PYTHON

A cousin of the Indian Rock Python, the Burmese variety is found in the savannas and low forests of Myanmar and neighboring Southeast Asian regions. It has a characteristic dark, arrow-shaped marking on its head and dark streaks through each eye.

Measuring twenty feet long, weighing in at several hundred pounds of brute muscle and bone, and with a body as thick as a steroided-out weightlifter's thigh, Burmese Python dwarfs not only his fellow snakes on the plane, but the humans, too.

He's the biggest, yes, but is he also the baddest? That depends on what you think is worse: being crushed to death or dying from toxic venom.

Burmese Python is a constrictor, which means that he engulfs his prey in his muscular coils and squeezes it to death. But he's no one-trick pony, for he can further subdue his victim by biting it and by clubbing it to insensibility with his massive head.

Being squeezed by a Burmese Python has a similar effect to being pulped by a hydraulic press, breaking every bone in a human body and rupturing all vital organs—so think twice before asking the big fellow for a hug.

Couldn't Happen to a Nicer Guy

Passengers stare, horrified, not at Paul, but at what's behind him.

TIFFANY: LOOK OUT!

Paul wheels around.

PAUL: Oh, God.

Burmese Python lunges and wraps around him, squeezing Paul until we hear organs bursting and bones snapping.

Snake Bite

Like vipers and boas, pythons also possess heat-seeking pits in their heads.

Because of their size and relative slowness, pythons hunt by luring their prey into an ambush. Coiled and still, motionless, the snake patiently hides in the brush beside a water hole or jungle trail, waiting for some unwary deer or pig or suchlike to come wandering along.

Throwing its coils around the prey, it squeezes it to death and swallows it whole.

Pythons ordinarily don't attack full-grown adult humans, though small children and pets are always in danger.

A rare example of a python attacking a full-grown human was recorded in Burma during World War II, when a jungle patrol came across a python with the legs and feet of a Japanese soldier protruding from its maw. The rest of the trooper was inside him.

Zapped

HARRIS: Wow. That's a nasty looking bite you've got there. Looks like you could use some anti-venom.

KRAITLER: In the fridge. Hurry!

HARRIS: Hurry? What for?

DR. PRICE: That was a South American Rattlesnake. Indigenous to Venezuela.

HARRIS: And in your expert opinion, how much time does he have to live?

DR. PRICE: About seven minutes.

Personality Profile
VENEZUELAN RATTLESNAKE

Poor Venezuelan Rattlesnake!

Pity this lively, engagingly lethal Venezuelan rattlesnake, who has to stay home and miss the party while the other snakes are packed off to the flying fang-fest that is Pacific Air Flight 121.

His North American Rattlesnake cousin is luckier and gets in on the fun, but he's stuck in his glass cage at the L.A. warehouse where exotic, illegally imported snakes are interned.

It's not fair. Venezuelan Rattlesnake is no less talented than his Yankee cousin, and no less deadly. The South American rattlesnake is stout and frequently distinguished by parallel markings on its neck and diamond-shaped markings on its back. The only rattlesnake found in much of the South American continent, it prefers dry grasslands and scrub brush, and shuns the rain forest.

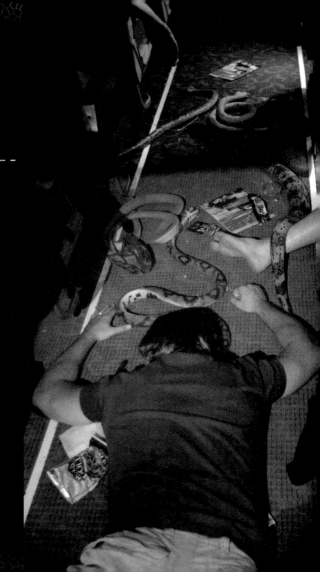

No Constitutional Right to Anti-Venom

Desperate for the anti-venom, Kraitler gives Harris a list of the kinds of snakes and number of them.

HARRIS: That's every snake on that plane?

KRAITLER: Yes.

HARRIS: Did Eddie Kim pay you to do this?

KRAITLER: YES! Now gimme the goddamn shot.

HARRIS: Or what? You gonna call the ACLU?

11 Best Defense

Life Raft

Sean and Tiffany inflate a life raft, using it to block the stairwell opening and stem the snake onslaught.

TIFFANY: It's supposed to be shark proof.

TROY: About now, sharks are sounding pretty good.

Personality Profile
GREEN MAMBA

It's not easy being green.

The green mamba is second only to the black mamba when it comes to being the deadliest snake in all Africa. When you're Number Two, you try harder.

Green mambas are tree-dwelling snakes that can grow to a length of six feet and make their home in the savannas of East Africa. Their favorite prey is birds and small mammals.

A squad of green mambas occupy the Flight 121 cockpit with the intent to hold it against all comers.

Who controls the cockpit, rules the plane. That's why Green Mamba and company are cavorting on top of the 747's instrument panel console like the damnedest hood ornaments you ever saw.

Nobody's taking over the controls if they have any say over it. Any passenger unlucky enough to fall afoul of their fangs must die.

Snake Bite

The green mamba is the world's only uniformly colored all-green snake. Other species of green snakes have some additional colorings or markings, such as striping, yellow or white undersides, brown or black bands, and the like. But the green mamba is green all over.

When you come to the tall grass in the green mamba's home turf, walk softly, friend. Better still, take the long way around.

Do or Die

Green mambas infest the cockpit.

CLAIRE: We have to get the snakes out of there.

FLYNN: All right . . . I've had it with these motherfuckin' snakes on this motherfuckin' plane. Everyone needs to strap in. I'm about to open some goddamn windows.

12 Coming In on a Fang and a Prayer

Meet the New Pilot

With the pilot and co-pilot dead, Troy steps up to fly the plane. He communicates via radio with Bradley at the LAX Air Control tower.

BRADLEY (gasps): Sir, are you telling me your only real flight time is at the controls of a video game?

TROY: It ain't a video game, it's a "flight simulator."

Deplaning

Claire hands Flynn her number.

> **CLAIRE:** Call me.

> **FLYNN:** Will do.

> **CLAIRE:** Tomorrow.

> **FLYNN:** First thing.

Surf's Up, Snakes Down

Flynn and Sean are in wetsuits, sitting on their boards in the water off Oahu.

> **SEAN:** Do you remember the first thing you ever told me?

> **FLYNN:** What the fuck has that got to do with anything?

> **SEAN:** What was the first thing you ever told me?

> **FLYNN:** Do as I say and you live.

> **SEAN:** Exactly! Now, it's your turn. Do as I say and *you* live! Relax—and paddle!